DISCARD

Teenage Refugees From
IRAN
Speak Out

IN THEIR OWN VOICES

Teenage Refugees From IRAN Speak Out

GINA STRAZZABOSCO

THE ROSEN PUBLISHING GROUP, INC.
NEW YORK

Published in 1995 by The Rosen Publishing Group, Inc.
29 East 21st Street, New York, New York 10010

First Edition
Copyright © 1995 by The Rosen Publishing Group, Inc.

All rights reserved. No part of this book may be reproduced in any form without permission in writing from the publisher, except by a reviewer.

Manufactured in the United States of America.

Library of Congress Cataloging-in-Publication Data

Strazzabosco, Gina.
  Teenage refugees from Iran speak out / Gina Strazzabosco. — 1st ed.
    p.   cm. — (In their own voices)
  Includes bibliographical references and index.
  ISBN 0-8239-1845-9
  1. Iranian American teenagers—Juvenile literature. 2. Refugees—United States—Juvenile literature. I. Title. II. Series.
E184.I5S77 1995
973'.04915—dc20
                                       94-41372
                                              CIP
                                               AC

Contents

	Introduction	7
1)	Sepi: The *Mojahedin*	20
2)	Marjan: Being Baha'i	26
3)	Reza: The Warmth of Family	32
4)	Mayam: Barred From University	38
5)	Evelyn: Sleeping in the Bathroom	44
6)	Vahid and Navid: One Planet, One People	50
7)	Anita: Saying the Shemah	54
	Glossary	61
	For Further Reading	62
	Index	63

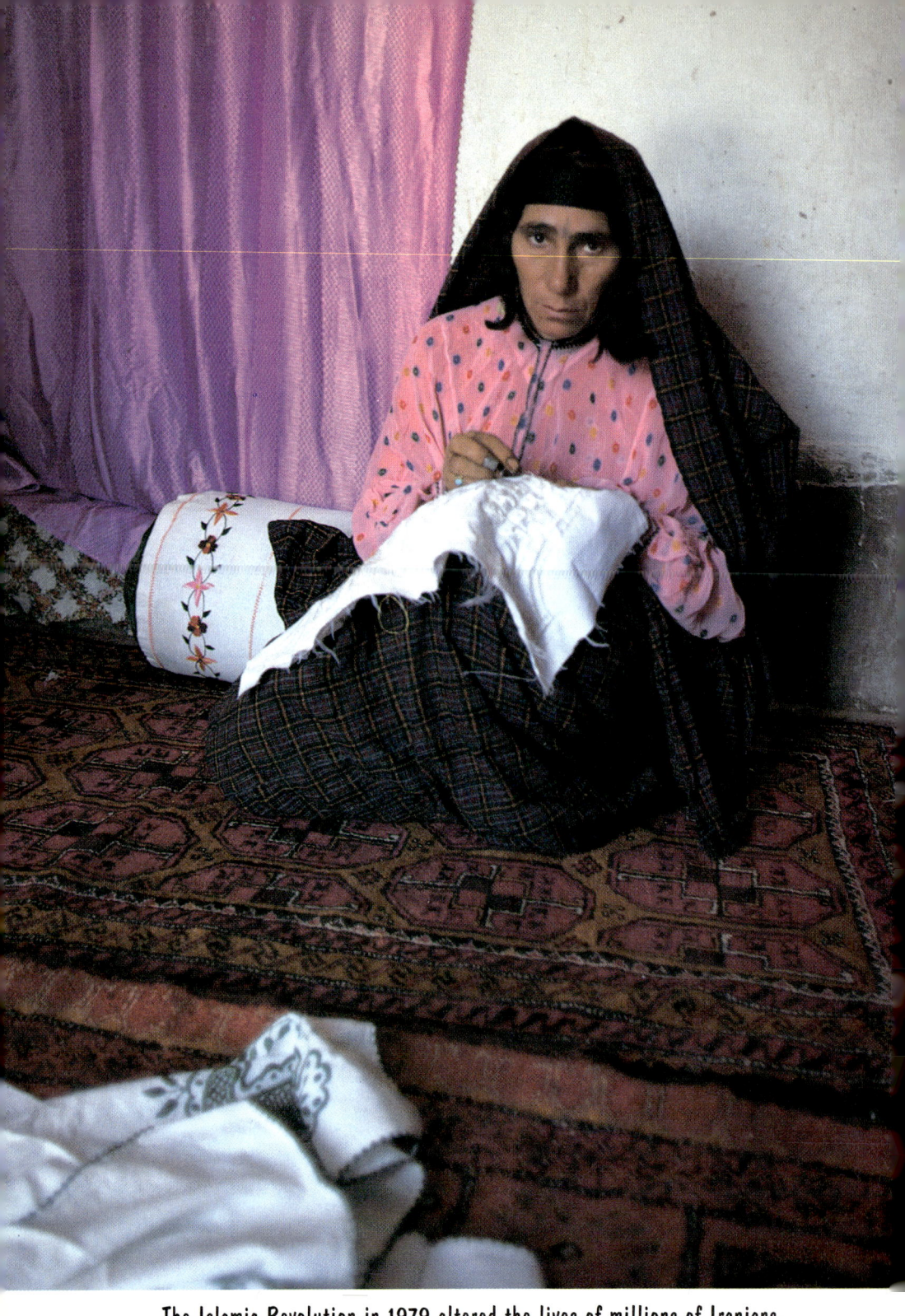
The Islamic Revolution in 1979 altered the lives of millions of Iranians.

INTRODUCTION

Iranian history stretches back nearly 2,500 years. Iran, once known as Persia, has at times been the center of vast empires extending through much of the Middle East. Today Iran is a single country in Southwest Asia, more than twice the size of Texas. Its population consists of Persians, Turkomans, Baluchis, Kurds, Afghanis, and Arabs.

The Islamic Revolution in 1979 and the events leading up to it caused hundreds of thousands of Iranians to flee their native country. Some feared for their lives. Others feared religious persecution.

The Islamic Revolution brought a sudden end to the monarchical rule that had been a feature of Iranian government for nearly 500 years. Iran's first empire, the Achaemenid Empire, was established by the sixth century BC. Its most powerful monarch was Darius I. The ruling dynasty changed only if it was conquered or overthrown. Many dynasties have ruled Iran.

The Arabs conquered Iran in AD 651. They brought with them the religion of Islam, replacing the indigenous Zoroastrian faith. From this point in Iran's history, religion and politics became inseparable. Every Persian ruler thereafter reigned

> **Zoroastrianism**
> Zoroastrianism was founded by Zoroaster, a Persian religious teacher. Its principles, dictated by religious writings called the Avesta, include belief in an afterlife and in the continuous struggle between the universal spirit of good and the spirit of evil, with good ultimately winning.

under some interpretation of the Islamic doctrine.

During the eleventh and twelfth centuries, the Arabs ruling Persia were defeated by the Seljuk Turks. The Seljuks created a bureaucracy that was the foundation for the Iranian government until the twentieth century. The Seljuks also revived the Islamic educational system and developed universities to train bureaucrats and religious officials. Persia was then conquered twice by Mongol warriors, Genghis Khan in the thirteenth century and Timur (Tamerlane or Timur the Lame) in the late fourteenth century.

During the sixteenth century, Shah Ismail, who ruled from 1502 to 1524, founded the Safavid Dynasty, which restored Persia as a political entity and established Shiism as the national religion. Prior to the sixteenth century, Persians had practiced Sunni Islam. Sunnis rely only on the direct teachings of Allah as revealed in the Koran, the *hadith,* and the *sunna.* About 8 percent of the Persian population in Iran still practices Sunni Islam.

The Safavid Dynasty was overthrown by its neighbor, Afghanistan, in 1722. Persian independence was restored in 1736 by the Afshar Dynasty,

> ### Islam
> Islam is the Muslim religion. It is monotheistic, meaning that its followers believe in one God, Allah. The founder and chief prophet of Islam is Muhammad. The majority of Iranians practice Shia Islam, or Shiism. Shiism teaches that the spiritual and secular or nonreligious leadership of the Islamic community should be with the direct descendants of Muhammad. These descendants are called Imams. Together they make up what is called the Imamate, or the governing force. According to Shiites, Imams are divinely protected against sin and error and have a perfect understanding of their sacred book of revelations, the Koran, as well as other powers. Besides the Koran, Shiite religious texts are interpretations of the *hadith* (sayings attributed to Muhammad) and the *sunna* (the model life shown by him), and the teachings of the Imams. In the absence of the Imam, certain others, particularly the *'ulama*, or religious scholars, can advise the community.

which was followed by the Zand Dynasty in 1750. This was overthrown by the Qajar Dynasty, which held the throne until 1925. The Qajars lacked the strong religious ties to the throne that previous rulers had had. That lack, combined with the discovery of petroleum and subsequent attempts by foreign countries to dominate that industry, caused social tensions and civil unrest.

In 1925, a strong leader, Reza Shah Pahlavi, took the throne from the Qajars and created the Pahlavi Dynasty. Reza Shah began a move toward modernization by uniting all of the independent groups of people living in Persia. He also instituted a nonreligious legal code and took possession of

The Western-oriented goals of Mohammed Reza Shah, left, were vastly different from the conservative Islamic goals of the Ayatollah Khomeini.

all religious income. He built secular schools, roads, hospitals, and the Trans-Iranian Railroad.

Reza Shah also promoted the rights of women. Up to this time, Iranian society practiced general public segregation of the sexes. Women wore a *chador,* or veil, in public or when males not related to them were in the house. In the Muslim tradition, women were confined to the home, where they managed the household and raised children. The Pahlavi government sought to promote desegregation between the sexes. It banned the *chador* in 1936 and encouraged mixed participation in many public gatherings.

It was at this point that Persia became Iran. In 1935, the Iranian government requested use of the older and correct name, Iran, meaning "Land of the Aryans," the people from whom Iranians are believed to be descended.

> **The Meaning of Aryan**
> The term Aryan was once used to categorize both a linguistic family and a hypothetical race. Scholars, struck by the similarities among ancient Indian languages such as Sanskrit and ancient European languages such as Latin and Greek, thought that there might once have been a group of people who were both Indian and European, or Indo-European. They believed that these Indo-Europeans had migrated into Southern Asia and Europe four million years ago. It was argued that northern Indians (who had a lighter skin color than southern Indians) and the peoples of Western Europe had descended from the same group, Aryans. Today, the term Aryan is used to designate a family of primarily Indian languages, including Bengali, Hindi, Punjabi, and Sinhalese.

Reza Shah was succeeded by his son, Mohammed Reza Shah Pahlavi, who continued on the course his father had begun. He launched what he called the White Revolution by beginning redistributing the land owned by the wealthy and the religious leaders. Mohammed Reza also expanded public education, restored internal order, revised the legal system, and fully emancipated women. Oil revenues helped to fund this rapid pace of modernization.

The general public overwhelmingly supported traditional Muslim values. Led by powerful Shia clergy, they opposed the modernization and reforms that Mohammed Reza had introduced. The clash of these groups led to tension and violence, which the Shah controlled with the help of his brutal secret police, the Savak.

The tension came to a head in 1978 when conservative Muslim protests led to violent riots. In November 1978, the Shah placed Iran under military rule. The protests continued, directed by the exiled Islamic fundamentalist leader Ayatollah Sayyid Ruhollah Musavi Khomeini. The Ayatollah had once been one of the six grand ayatollahs of the Shiite Muslims. He was exiled in 1963 for taking part in religious demonstrations against the Shah. The Ayatollah wanted to depose the royal regime and create a traditional Islamic society with laws and values taken directly from the Koran.

In an attempt to compromise with the protesters, the Shah lifted military rule on January 6, 1979. However, the people demanded more. Demonstrations calling for the Shah's exile were held. On January 16, the Shah went into exile. The Ayatollah Khomeini took power on February 1. On February 12, Iran was proclaimed an Islamic republic. Hundreds of the Shah's supporters and alleged members of the Savak, as well as members of many other groups believed to have opposed Khomeini's regime, were arrested, tried, and executed. Khomeini initiated policies to reverse the Westernization of Iran. A new constitution established a parliamentary form of government with an elected president and a parliament consisting of one legislative branch, the *Sharia* (Islamic law) as the basis of the legal system, and a council of guardians,

ENGLISH TRANSLATION FROM FARSI:
A wise person thinks before acting.

primarily religious leaders. The constitution gave authority to a supreme religious guide, or *faghi*. Khomeini was named *faghi* for life.

The 1979 revolution and institution of Islamic law affected many aspects of Iranian society. The overwhelming majority of Iranians, at least 90 percent, are Muslims who follow Shia Islam. But even the least religious Iranians were forced to follow strict Islamic codes of behavior. All Western customs were banned. Laws were enacted restricting women in public life. *Hejab*, or properly modest attire for women, became a major issue. Women were required to cover their hair and skin, with the exception of hands and faces, whenever they appeared in public. For most women, for whom

Women in Iran are required to cover everything but their hands and faces.

wearing the *chador* was a longtime tradition, this law had little impact. But it was controversial among modernized and nonreligious women. School textbooks were rewritten to place greater emphasis on religion and traditional values. Everything from schools to beaches were once again segregated by sex.

Khomeini's regime sought to eliminate those who opposed the strict Islamic regime. Many were executed. Certain religious groups, particularly Baha'is and Jews, were persecuted mercilessly. Thousands of people fled the country. Many were granted refugee status in other countries, including Israel and the United States.

Khomeini's regime was antagonistic toward the United States because of its long support of the

The Religion of Baha'i

The Baha'is are the largest religious minority in Iran, numbering between 150,000 and 300,000. They were also one of the most persecuted groups during Khomeini's reign.

Baha'i is a relatively young religion that originated in Iran. Its roots lie in Babism, a branch of Shia Islam. Baha'is believe in the unity of humans and religion, in sexual equality, in universal education and world peace, and in the introduction of a world calendar and an international language. Khomeini's regime considered Baha'is to be heretics because their beliefs deviate from orthodox Islam. They are considered "unprotected infidels," a non-Islamic group whose beliefs are not recognized by the constitution, as are Christians, Jews, and Zoroastrians. Baha'is were also believed to have supported the Shah, despite the fact that political participation is forbidden within the Baha'i religion.

For these and other reasons, Baha'is are denied their basic human rights in Iran. They are not allowed to leave the country. Their only hope is to escape. Between the Islamic Revolution in 1979 and 1985, 195 Baha'is died by execution, in prison, by assassination, by being beaten, stoned, or burned to death by mobs. Some have disappeared and are presumed dead. Seven hundred Baha'is have been held in prison without being charged.

While the plight of the Baha'is has improved considerably since the intervention of the United Nations Commission on Human Rights, they are still denied the right to express their religious belief freely. All Baha'i holy places and historical sites remain confiscated and many have been destroyed.

The unpredictable and often brutal regime in Iran led to a large number of refugees.

Shah. In October 1979, the Shah was allowed to enter the U.S. for medical treatment. Conservative Iranian college students seized the U.S. embassy in Tehran on November 4, 1979, and took hostages, 62 of whom were U.S. citizens. The militants vowed to stay in the embassy until the Shah was returned to Iran for trial. This was the beginning of a long international crisis during which the U.S. broke diplomatic relations with Iran. The hostages were finally released in January 1981.

The ruling Islamic Party, increasingly dissatisfied with President Abolhassan Bani Sadr, who was elected in January 1980, declared him unfit for office in June 1981. In the weeks following Bani

> **The Iran-Contra Affair**
>
> The Iran-Iraq war, the U.S. hostage crisis, and links to terrorist activities led to an almost complete isolation of Iran from other countries. The U.S. publicly stated that it would no longer negotiate with terrorists and an embargo had been placed on arms sales to Iran. Yet former U.S. National Security Advisor Robert McFarlane met secretly with the Iranian government in November 1986 to negotiate an end to Iranian support of terrorist acts in return for the sale of spare parts for Iranian weapons. The money Iran paid for the weapons parts was used secretly and illegally to fund pro-*contra* military efforts in Nicaragua, when the Reagan Administration hope to see an end to Sandinista rule. The information was revealed to the U.S. public in May 1987, and the scandal that followed was called the Iran-Contra Affair.

Sadr's dismissal, a new wave of executions began. His successor, Muhammad Ali Rajai, was assassinated later that year by an unknown political group. Hojatolislam Ali Khamenei was elected president in 1981 and reelected in 1985.

After Khomeini's death on July 3, 1989, Khamenei was elected to succeed him as supreme religious leader. Hojatolislam Hashemi Rafsanjani, speaker of the parliament, became president after July 1989. He was reelected in June 1993.

Despite the recent conflicts, Iran has a long and tumultuous history. Its political and religious atmosphere has caused thousands of people to

549-330 BC The Achaemenid Empire, the world's first empire, extended from the Aegean Sea to the Indus River. Its Persian kings created institutions such as the postal system and coinage. Zoroastrianism became the most widely practiced religion during this time.

329-323 BC Persia was one of the many countries Alexander the Great ruled until he died.

651-1055 The Arabs ruled Persia for several hundred years. They introduced the religion of Islam.

13th Century Mongol conqueror Genghis Khan ruled Persia.

14th Century Timur, also known as Timur the Lame, conquered Persia in a five-year war campaign.

16th Century The Safavid Dynasty, founded by Shah Ismail in 1502, established Shia Islam, or Shiism, as the official religion.

1722-1736 Afghanistan conquered Persia; its rule lasted only 14 years.

1736-1750 The Afshar Dynasty was ruled by a despot, Nadir Shah. He reestablished Persian independence.

1794-1925 The Qajar Dynasty was unable to control the country or to save it from foreign domination once oil was discovered in 1908.

1925-1941 Reza Shah Pahlavi assumed the throne in 1925. He began to modernize Iran. He turned the throne over to his son to avoid complications with the United States and Great Britian over their interests in Iran's oil.

1941-1979 Mohammed Reza Shah Pahlavi proceeded on the path of modernization, facing opposition from Islamic fundmentalists such as the exiled Ayatollah Ruhollah Khomeini. Mohammed Reza was forced into exile in 1979.

1979-1989 Ayatollah Ruhollah Khomeini established an absolute Islamic government, naming himself supreme religious ruler for life. Upon his death in 1989, then President Hojatolislam Ali Khamenei was named supreme religious ruler and remains so today.

Iranians protested what they considered to be the fascist government under Khomeini's rule.

leave, many in fear for their lives. One thing these refugees share with those who choose to remain in Iran is a strong sense of culture and heritage. The pain of having to leave their native country has not destroyed their pride in being Persian. Most Persian refugees are waiting for a time when they can return to their beloved country.

*   *   *

Some of the teenagers interviewed for this book asked that their photographs not be used. In some cases they have done so in order to protect relatives who remain in Iran. They fear that their families may be in danger if their identities are discovered. In all cases, we have used only the students' first names in order to protect their privacy.◆

At the age of sixteen, **Sepi** is a bright young woman who is full of life. She has been in New York for four years and speaks flawless English. Her most prominent feeling about Iran is fear.

SEPI
THE *MOJAHEDIN*

When I was four years old we moved from Tehran, Iran, to Germany. We lived there until I was twelve, and then we moved to New York. Now we live in Bayside, Queens.

I remember what it was like living in Tehran. I remember my grandparents, and I have many pictures. Even when I was young, I had to wear the head cover when we went outside. My mom wasn't allowed to wear any makeup. Once she had makeup on, and the police told her to go clean up. My mom couldn't stay there anymore. It was too scary.

In Iran, they force people to go into the army. They wanted to take my dad into the army, but we moved to Germany. My dad always wanted to come to the U.S. But first we had to go to Germany, where we stayed as refugees.

I'm Muslim. My older sister went to school in Iran, and she told me that religion was the only

Khomeini dictated the lives of everyone in Iran. Children were made to wear military uniforms in celebration of Army Day ceremonies.

thing they taught in schools. It was all about being Muslim. My parents were never prejudiced. They had Jewish friends in Iran.

My parents didn't agree with the government. When Khomeini came, he told lies about what he was going to do for the people of Iran, and everyone believed him. Everyone was protesting against the Shah and wanted Khomeini in power because of what he promised. The Shah cared more about being friends with other countries than fixing his own country. There was a lot of poverty in Iran. The Shah never tried to fix it. That was how the Persian people saw it, so when Khomeini said he would fix Iran, that he cared about his own people first, people believed him. But when he came into power we found out that all the things he said were lies.

At first, people were given the choice to wear the traditional head coverings and pray. Then he forced them to follow the old traditions. No one could have their own ideas. Everything he did was for the Muslim religion. "We are killing these people in the name of the Muslim religion." It was all lies. My parents are Muslim, and they don't agree with him at all.

Khomeini had one of Mom's brothers and her sister killed because they protested against him. Mom's brother was only seventeen when he was killed, and her sister was nineteen.

There are groups who don't like the way Khomeini treats people in Iran. Those people call themselves the *mojahedin.* There are a lot of them here in the States. They fight wars with Iran to try to get their country back. My mom is part of that group here. Khomeini considered these protesters terrorists. The *mojahedin* want people to have their own ideas, have their own country. They will have the leader of the *mojahedin* lead Iran if they get it back. He believes in people doing what they want to: If you want to wear the head covering, go ahead. If you don't want to pray, don't do it.

People don't like the *mojahedin* because they fight with Iran, with Persian people. But how can you get your country back if you don't fight for it? It is the only way. We agree with the *mojahedin.*

Because of my mother's brother and sister, she isn't actively involved with the *mojahedin*, but she totally agrees with them. She supports them financially. There are all kinds of people of different religions, Muslims and Jews, who care and support the *mojahedin.* I asked my friend's mom (she's Jewish) about it, but she's scared to be a part of it. She didn't even want to talk about it. It is difficult to be *mojahedin* or to support them because Khomeini's men are looking for you all the time. They'll kill you if they find you. Even in the States.

The only thing I want is for Persian people to be free in their own country and not be forced to do anything they don't like to do. I want it to be a democratic country.

My parents want to go back to Iran. I've spent much of my life outside of it. I lived in Germany for a long time and speak German fluently. We went to Germany because they were taking a lot of refugees and it was an easy way to get out. We left Germany because my dad's family are here and he always wanted to move here.

We had to change many things, like our ages, on our passports in order to leave Iran. If you are male and fifteen years or older you are not allowed to leave, because they want you in the army. My dad lied and said he needed to see a doctor in Germany.

They took our Persian passports when we left Iran. There's no possibility for my parents to go back and visit. But my sisters and I can get new

Family and culture are important to Persians, both in Iran and abroad. Here a young girl weaves a Persian rug in the traditional manner.

passports. My sisters want to go for the summer. I would never go back. You never know what will happen to you there. There is no law. It's really scary; if they don't like you, you're dead. I think my parents will go back to Iran no matter what happens. I think most Persian people will go back.

We are the only family that I know of who moved from Iran and still know how to speak, write, and read Farsi. It is important to my mom that we don't forget our language. I consider Germany or the United States to be my homeland. I'm scared of Iran, of what goes on there. I would never want to go back there.◆

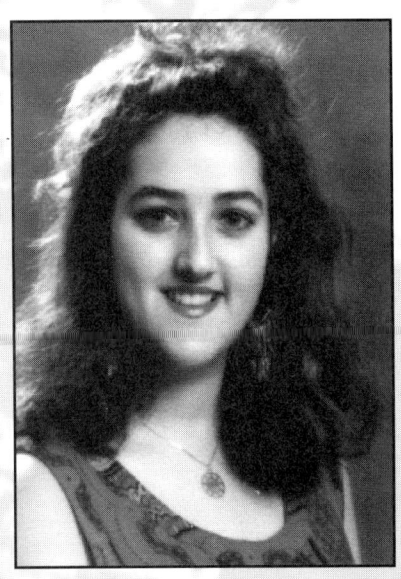

Marjan is nineteen years old. She is an intelligent, well-spoken young woman of Baha'i faith. According to Marjan, Baha'is consider themselves to be citizens of the world, and as such, must work for the unity and exaltation of humanity. The Baha'is in Iran have suffered much persecution at the hands of the Shiite Muslims in power. Thousands have been imprisoned, hundreds executed, and many have left the country. Marjan's father was the victim of such persecution.

MARJAN
BEING BAHA'I

I was four years old when I left Iran. I remember my home and my family. My mother brought us to the United States because we have family here. I have two sisters and a brother. My mom raised us, because my father was killed in 1981.

My father was arrested in Tehran for being a Baha'i because he was part of the local Spiritual Assembly of Tehran. The governing body of the Baha'i faith consists of three levels of administrative order called the Spiritual Assembly: the local level, the national level, and the international level. My father was on the local Spiritual Assembly. In 1981, my father was executed for being a Baha'i, as were a lot of other people in the community. They are still being persecuted in Iran.

The Baha'is have been persecuted ever since the coming of the prophet of the faith. In history this has always been the case. The first Christians were persecuted and put to death. The first Jews were, the first Muslims were. It happened with the birth of the Baha'i faith as well, which was 150 years ago. Now, especially since the Islamic Revolution in 1979, it has started up again.

Baha'is believe in all of the religions of the past. We believe in Judaism, Christianity, Islam, Buddhism, and all the other major religions of the world. But we believe that they came at different times. We believe there is one God, and He sends us different messengers at different times. As we mature, God sends us a new messenger with new social teachings but the same underlying spiritual teachings that have been true for all of these major religions. We believe that Baha Allah is the prophet for this day and age who has the teachings that are right for this era, this time. Persian Muslims obviously don't accept that. The Shiites are waiting for the coming of a certain twelfth Imam.

The Baha'i community in the United States is extremely strong. The faith, statistically, is the second most widespread religion, next to Christianity. It is the fastest growing religion.

The Baha'i faith is a way of life. It directs every breath I take. My activities outside of school are to promote the exaltation of the human race. For my own spiritual being, I pray every day. There is no special church or anything, but every nineteen days the Baha'i community of Santa Monica, for example, which is where I live, comes together

Although many of the once magnificent Baha'i temples in Iran have been destroyed by the Ayatollah Khomeini's regime, Baha'i temples can be found throughout the world. This temple is in Sydney, Australia.

Two men playing traditional Persian instruments.

for what we call a feast. It's a spiritual feast, and its purpose is unity within the community.

There are laws in the Baha'i faith as in every religion, such as prayer, a month of fasting, things like that. If we do these things, we will grow spiritually. These are all found in the *Kitab-i-aqdas,* "The Most Holy Book." It was written by Baha Allah, not handed down through generations. Over one hundred volumes were written by the prophet himself.

My mother reminisces about the past and the times when it was better in Iran. It was better before the revolution. Life was a lot easier for everybody. But this is what has happened and we accept it and it's okay. The revolution is what caused the Baha'i faith to spread so vastly in such a short time.

My family have become citizens of the United States. We don't believe in nationalism. I was born in Iran, as all my family were, so we are Persians, we are Americans, but we are also citizens of the world.

The youth of today should really focus on our future because the youth will be in the forefront of the battle against all the things that are happening to the world: racism, prejudice, sexism. They have to work for the principles that will cause the station of humanity to be exalted.

My favorite quotation from Baha Allah is: Ye are the leaves of one branch and the fruits of one tree. ◆

Although **Reza**, sixteen, enjoys some aspects of living in the United States, he believes strongly that he and many of his fellow Persian refugees will return to their homeland once the regime that Ayatollah Khomeini instituted has been replaced. He has a passion for his culture.

REZA
THE WARMTH OF FAMILY

I am sixteen. I live in West Hills, California. I have been in the United States for nine years. Life over there is better than here because of the warmth you feel from your family. All of my family are still there. We were always at each other's houses. Here it is not like that. We have only our uncle here, no other family.

The revolution was the people kicking the Shah out and Khomeini taking power. The people were unhappy with the Shah. They believed that he cared more about himself and his family than the country. The Shah and his people were building themselves big castles and weren't doing much for the country. The people wanted change so they revolted. They didn't know what would happen when Khomeini came. The Shah was too nice and held back his army. If he had let his army suppress the revolution, none of the problems we have now would have happened. When Khomeini came, he told a bunch of lies. People believed him and thought life would be better. He didn't do any of the things he said he would do.

My parents said that during the revolution there were fights outside all the time. People were getting shot. They would throw fire bombs and set things on fire. We also had a curfew; we couldn't go on the street after a certain hour. We would go on the roof and watch what was happening.

My dad was an actor in Iran, and Mom was a nurse. When Khomeini came, commercials or movies weren't allowed. Dad lost his job.

Dad isn't one to take things lying down. We left Iran because he couldn't stand what was going on. One of the last things I remember was being at my grandma's house. We heard a gunshot. Dad came running in, saying that they just shot some kid, maybe about my age. One of Khomeni's guards shot him in the head because he was handing out flyers. Dad stood in the street cursing Khomeini. His friends who had a store on that street pulled him inside and calmed him down. If the guards had caught my dad saying that stuff, they would have done the same to him.

We finally got our visas. A year later, my dad bought someone else's passport and was able to leave Iran.

We came to California to be with my uncle. We told Immigration about our situation, and we got our refugee green cards. They had told us in Iran

Persians dealt with war for many years—the ten-year war with Iraq and the Islamic Revolution that followed.

that the ground in the United States was so clean you could kiss it. It wasn't all that clean, but we liked it. Life is much more convenient here. Under Khomeni, we had food coupons and had to stand in line for two hours or more just to get things like oil or butter. Here you just walk into a supermarket and everything is there for you.

I'm Muslim. I am really into my religion. I fast, I pray. We fast for forty days for Ramadan. Some people say we celebrate Ramadan because that's when our God, Allah, gave the Koran to Muhammad. Others say it's because Muhammad was being starved by someone and we must go through the same thing he did. We get up at around four a.m. to eat and pray before sunrise; then we eat again after sundown, around six. We can't eat or drink anything, even water, during the day. It's hard when we're in school. You run a mile in physical education and you come back and can't drink any water.

Most of my friends here are Persian. My family are not citizens. We are refugees. I consider myself to be Persian. Our family have always stayed together and kept our culture. We never adapted to the American world.

Being Persian to me means that we are all down for our country. My friends and I never want to become Americans or change our names. Our country is so beautiful that we don't need to do that. No family has the warmth of a Persian family and home. The beautiful cities, the agriculture, and the architecture could never exist here. We have so much history.

There are things that I do like about the U.S. The convenience, for one. I like it because I have friends here, and there is a better environment and better jobs. It's freer, but it may be too free because not everything is good here. The country is not doing too well right now. There is so much crime.

I plan on going back to Iran someday, if it gets better. The Khomeini regime must be replaced for the country to get better. We'll wait and see what happens. You can't trust anyone there right now. My mom and sister are going back to visit soon. My relatives there say that the prices have gone up so much. Women have no rights. Neither do the men, but women are treated worse. Kids have to go into the army. They say that the kids must be eighteen, but who knows? People go to Iran from here and Khomeini's government keeps them in Iran. The things they do are terrible. But I still love my country.

I'd just like to say to any Persian readers, always stay with your own culture. Stay Persian. Don't sell your country out for any other country because your country was a beautiful country, and I'm sure it always will be because God likes that country. Don't give up hope.◆

Mayam left her mother and sister in Iran less than a year ago. She and her father arrived in Chicago to live with an uncle. She is Baha'i and has suffered many of the consequences of being a member of a religious minority in Iran.

Mayam is currently working as a translator at the Baha'i National Center in Chicago. She plans to attend college next fall.

MAYAM
BARRED FROM UNIVERSITY

I have been in the United States for about eight months. I came with my father. My mother and my sister are still in Iran. I was able to come here with my father because my uncle, who lives here in Chicago, had a green card. That allowed my father to get an immigration visa, and I could come along because I was under twenty-one years old. My sister is older and couldn't use this benefit. My mother and sister will join us later, but we have no idea when.

I graduated from high school three years ago, but I was barred from entering university because of my religion. I used to be a very good student, the first student in the whole high school. But still they didn't even let me take the entrance exam.

All students are forced to wear traditional Muslim clothing and learn about Islam in school regardless of their religion.

There are many other things in Iran that made us decide to leave. I could talk a lot about the problems that Baha'is suffered. In general, it is difficult to communicate with people outside of Iran. You are in a very closed atmosphere that does not let you grow. That's the feeling I had. That's the feeling that many other youths who are not Baha'i also have, but being a Baha'i, I encountered other difficulties. For example, I could not find a good job. I used to go to an English Institute to learn English. I almost finished my studies. They have teacher training courses, and many students are chosen to participate in those courses and eventually teach in the institute. I took all the courses, but when the time came they did not hire me because I was a Baha'i. Government departments never hire a Baha'i, and the private sector is afraid to do it.

I had religious classes every day, but very secretly. Baha'is get together and study the teachings and try to deepen their understanding and knowledge. Sometimes I took French classes, which were also held in a Baha'is home secretly. Most of the time I had to stay at home. Sometimes I went out with friends to the cinema or shopping, but when you left the house you had to be very careful. You had to watch out for the revolutionary guards on the streets who checked your Islamic uniform and such things. If I went out with my friends, and we were late by ten minutes or so, our parents worried that the guards had made trouble for us. Nobody feels comfortable in Iran. You always have to be careful not to get into trouble, especially if you are minority. For not having a complete uniform, if you are a Baha'i, they may keep you in prison for several days.

There are two TV channels in Iran. Both have about eight hours of programming a day. They rarely have movies; there is not much choice. But you can use a VCR. There are many videotapes, but they are considered illegal. You can handle this by finding someone to give them to you. There are American movies and Japanese movies. When they are not showing movies on TV, they show old detective shows or other serials. I watched one here, about Miss Marple, that they used to show in Iran. It was considered the best program, because all the others were very bad. They also show some movies produced in Iran about historical events.

I like being here because there is so much freedom. I can go to university. There is not so much religious prejudice here, so you really feel free. At the same time, it's not my country. There are many cultural differences between people here and people in my country. I should adjust, but it's a little bit hard for me. I should learn the language much better. When I translate words I want to say from the Farsi, it means something totally different in English. Just knowing the English words doesn't mean you know English.

The first thing I noticed here was that when you walk down the street, people say "Hi" to each other. But in a city like Tehran, when you walk down the street you do not greet anyone else. In Iran, people eat with a spoon and fork. Here they eat with a knife and fork. When you first come, you don't know these things, but little by little you learn.

I'm planning to go to university for a very long time. I can't go back to Iran easily because I do not have my passport. America is a nice place, a very good place, but it's hard to get used to. It takes time to feel comfortable, especially when you know that you have no way to go back to your country.

Culture varies in different parts of Iran. For instance, major cities are very modern, whereas people in the more remote areas live in the traditional ways.

I consider myself Baha'i over being Iranian. I think that if we consider ourselves by nationalities we are not united. It is better to consider ourselves as human beings. I think nationality is of no importance. It is a fact that I am from Iran; I'm not proud of that, I'm not sad about that. In the case of my religion, I am happy that I am a Baha'i, but that does not mean that I am proud of it. I have respect for all human beings and consider them equal. We should put aside everything that does not express unity. I would like to be considered a human being, not a Baha'i, not an Iranian.◆

Evelyn is an intelligent, highly motivated young woman. She vividly remembers scenes from Iran, including many nights spent hiding out during bombings that occurred during the 1979 Revolution. She is happy to be in the United States, but acknowledges that it is difficult to live in two worlds, that of her native culture and the less restrictive American culture.

EVELYN
SLEEPING IN THE BATHROOM

I am seventeen. I've been living in the United States for eight years. I went to an Orthodox Jewish private school until fourth grade. I remember everything about Iran. I remember my house, my elementary school, the playgrounds, the smell of the flowers where we used to live. I remember the snow, something we don't have here in California.

The hardest thing about living in Iran was during the war, which started in 1977. They were throwing bombs at us, mostly at night. We lived in an apartment building, and people came to see what part of the house was the safest to stay in during the bombings. Our bathroom turned out to be the safest place; we slept there whenever they bombed. A siren went off when the bombs began. At two or three o'clock people from the whole building would come to our bathroom and it was a very small bathroom. Those were the bad nights.

The Jewish population in Iran has dwindled because of discrimination. Mothers escort their children to school to protect them from other children's taunts.

My family decided to leave Iran and come to the United States near the end of the war.

We changed our names on our passports to a neighbor's because we are Jewish and Jews were not able to leave Iran easily. Then we flew here. This was dangerous because you had to go through checkpoints where government officials would question you. You had to pretend that you were a totally different person. I was nine years old, but my passport said I was a six-year-old Muslim girl. My little brother had to pass as a girl because that's what the passport said. They checked our whole bodies to make sure we weren't taking more money or gold than was allowed. That was the hardest part.

I miss Iran. I don't think I can go back, but if I could, I'd like to visit for a week or so, no more. It would've been easier to grow up over there than here. Here there are dress codes, you have to have a car, you have to have certain shoes. It's not like that over there. It's just simple. You enjoy your life. The littlest thing makes you happy.

I'm in high school, but I take classes at a community college. I'm taking English there now. My English is not good. I'm dyslexic, so I'm taking these classes that will help me in college later.

I consider myself one hundred percent Persian because my parents are, my grandparents are, and so are all the people I hang around with. It's really hard to live in two worlds at once. In my house you have to be Persian; you have to speak Farsi. But when I go outside, everyone talks about freedom, freedom of speech, why everyone has to be equal. I go to school and they tell me that men and women have to be equal, and then I come home and my parents treat me and my brother totally different because that's the way it was in Iran. He's allowed to go out and come home any time he wants. He can go on vacations for a couple of days with no problem. Just because he's a guy, he can do anything he wants. That's one thing that bothers me about my parents being Iranian in California.

I'm allowed to date, but only a certain kind of guy. He has to be older, he has to be Jewish, he has to be Persian, he has to be from a good family. My parents have to approve of him. I'd rather not date than have to deal with all these restrictions. I was seeing someone for a whole month. He was Persian, he was Jewish, he was older than me. I had a long talk with my parents last Sunday, and they said I had to break up with him because his family wasn't good enough. If I ever wanted to get serious, it wouldn't work between us. And there goes a very nice guy.

I think I'll raise my kids pretty much the way my parents have raised me. I'll have my daughter date only Jewish Persian guys, I hope. Even though it's been so difficult for me, I know it's not a bad thing. I know my parents want the best for me. They asked me to break up with my boyfriend. It was for the best. I knew his family wasn't good. He fought with his mom twenty-four hours a day. My parents discovered that he had eight brothers and sisters and none of them got along. If they can't get along, how could he and I get along? My parents are always looking to the future.

One thing I like about being Persian is the respect that we have for others. The respect that I have for adults is totally different than my friends'. You're sitting in a room and an adult walks in: You definitely get up. It's a habit I've had since I was a kid. In Iran you talked to a grown-up and to your friend in different ways. In the Persian language, you can talk with respect so much more easily than you can in English. I think that there is no respect in the English language.

Many refugees miss the familiarity of their homeland.

Americans are fun people. They live for today, not for tomorrow. Persian people are always thinking about the future.

My mom is an American citizen. I want to be a citizen one day. It's one of my dreams to be a citizen somewhere, to be part of a country. I have to choose a country, and I can't choose Iran, so I might as well choose here. ◆

Landing in Memphis, Tennessee, along with their parents, **Vahid**, left, and **Navid** took their chances when they left Iran in hopes of finding better conditions elsewhere in the world. As Baha'is in Iran, they were faced with the choice of denying their faith or leaving their country. Even living in the north, away from the most brutal abuse, the family felt the Muslim oppression of their religion. They chose freedom and have been living in the United States for four years.

VAHID AND NAVID
ONE PLANET, ONE PEOPLE

I was fifteen and Vahid was twelve when we came to the United States. We lived in the north of Iran, in Marzandaran, by the Caspian Sea.

Sari, where we lived, was a small city compared to Tehran. The weather was really nice, like here in Tennessee. We had the four seasons there; it was never too cold or too hot.

The school system is different in Iran. After the revolution, they separated the boys' and girls' schools. We had courses in mathematics, science (biology, chemistry, zoology), Arabic as our foreign language, English, history, geography, physical education, religion. We studied Islam in school. Studies about Islam did not conflict with our own studies of the Baha'i religion. We believe in all prophets of God, so we didn't have any trouble studying Islam. The problem was with the Islamic revolution. They wanted us to convert to Islam. They wanted Islamic people in the country. They started to bother us at school. They didn't let us have Baha'i classes, and they arrested and imprisoned us if we had meetings. Muslims called us names. They would say, "You are not of God. You are dogs; you are dirty."

My parents were working for the government. Everything in Iran is government owned. They were fired after the revolution because of their religion. All Baha'is were fired.

We are more fortunate than most Baha'is. Our parents were not hurt physically. The guards tried to escort us sometimes, but we were never hurt or placed in prison. None of our family has died because of being Baha'i. Some people were imprisoned and killed because of their religion.

Our father began to work for some engineers in private companies. After a few months, the government found out about that too. They threatened that if our father wasn't fired, they would make trouble. After that, there was no way our father could work.

We couldn't fly out of the country. That privilege was taken from us. Many of our relatives had escaped and gone to Pakistan for two and sometimes up to four years. Then they could go wherever they were sent. We escaped and went to Pakistan too. We stayed there for fifteen months waiting for the next opening for refugees. The way we lived in Pakistan was real primitive. We had only a room and sixteen people were living in it. There was no air conditioning, no refrigeration, no hot water to take a bath in. It was real hard.

We decided to come to the United States because it is economically developed. Also English is spoken here. I knew English because we had studied it. We ended up in Tennessee because we were sponsored by a Christian church in Nashville.

There are about one hundred fifty Baha'i families in Nashville. Every nineteen days we have a feast. As foretold by our prophet founders, we gather and socialize and get to know each other. We also talk about problems of the Baha'i community. Each meeting has three sections. There is the time when we say prayers. Then there's the administration time when we talk about problems and teachings. Then we have the consultation section, when we talk about how to improve the Baha'i community and also about how we can create a better world. Our principle is oneness of humankind, oneness of religion, and oneness of God, universal peace. After the formal sections, we have a social time. The person who sponsors the meeting serves the guests, and we sit and talk and find out about each other. The Baha'i community is really close.

We just became citizens of the United States. For the Baha'is, there is only one country, and that is the world. We think of the world as our country, as our homeland.

We are both going to the University of Tennessee at Knoxville to study pre-med. We will become doctors, hopefully, and work to save our community. That is what we are here for. ◆

On an average day, **Anita** looks like any number of New York  teenagers. Oversized demin clothes, hair tightly pulled away from her face, a bit of a swagger in her walk. But as she begins to talk, there emerges a self-assured, highly perceptive young woman who has adjusted well to her emigration.

7
ANITA
SAYING THE SHEMAH

My name is Anita. I am sixteen years old. I came to the United States when I was nine-and-a-half. I was born in Tehran and I am Jewish. Practicing Judaism is very hard there. I am trying to be religious now.

There are three kids in my family, my mom, and my dad. My parents wanted to leave Iran for seven years. It took a very long time because things kept coming up. Khomeini came into power, my dad's business was doing well, then my parents couldn't sell the house. Then, because we are Jewish, we had trouble getting visas to travel. Mom pulled some strings and got us out. We went to Italy for four months to get our visas. There is a corporation called Hayan that helps people who want to go to the United States and gets them visas. We had to tell the Iranian officials that we were going on vacation. I remember I was crying

Some parents paid a lot of money to send their children to refugee houses in Germany. The children cover their faces fearing retaliation on their families still in Iran if they are identified.

because we had to leave Dad behind for a year. They asked me why I was crying if we were just going on vacation. I told them I was going to miss my dad. They said, "But aren't you going to see him soon?" I said yes, and stopped crying.

It took a year to sell our house and all our belongings. Dad had to go undercover to leave Iran. He drove his car to Turkey and then to Italy. I think he grew a beard and told everyone he was Muslim.

Life under Khomeini was very hard. We had to stand in line for food coupons. Women have to cover themselves with a *maghneah* (head covering) and *rupush* (gown). Men can't wear bicycle shorts or tank tops, but they have more freedom. Once Mom was driving on the highway and her hair covering fell down to her shoulders. She was so glad. She said that the police officers could do whatever they wanted but she was glad not to be covered.

Another time Mom had just gotten a manicure and pedicure. We went out with my cousin's wife. The cops pulled us over and told Mom to go with them. She said no. They gave her nail polish remover and told her to wipe the nail polish off. My aunt said, "But she just got a manicure and she's going to a party!" But the cops made her take it off anyway. That night the husbands said, "I told you so."

The first school I went to in Tehran was Jewish, but when Khomeini came to power, the Muslims took over the school and we couldn't say the Jewish prayer, Shemah. I remember my Jewish teacher used to have someone stand by the door to watch for the principal and vice-principal who used to walk down the halls. We would take out our Bibles and read, but when they came, we would quickly put them away. They wanted us to learn about Muhammad and how the world began. It's different from Judaism. It starts out the same, but then it goes in a different direction.

On Thursdays, all the Jews stood outside in line and you got to say the Shemah and that was about it. Part of what they were doing was trying to convert you. Our teacher, who was supposed to teach us about Muhammad, was Jewish and told us not to listen to what they said. She used to stand in front of the class in tears. There are some parts of my childhood that I will never forget, and that is one of them.

Before he married my mom, my dad worked and went to college in the United States. He went back to Iran, married Mom, and worked in a corporation. His brother lived in the U.S. My dad sent money and gold to his brother to hold for him, because he knew he was going to come back one day. You weren't supposed to send gold and money from Iran, so Mom would open the bottom of toothpaste containers and put gold in there. Sometimes she would sew money or gold pieces in the seams of towels or clothes. My dad's brother bought us a house with all that money.

Despite the destruction and violence Khomeini subjected his people to, this 1986 photograph reflects the support he still found among the citizens.

I was happy that we were leaving Iran, but I did not know much about where we were going. All I knew was that I was going to miss my dad. Mom tells me that whenever I saw people with their fathers I used to curse them, I was so upset.

When we came to the United States we stopped in New York for twenty-one days. Then we went to California to stay with my mom's relatives until my dad got here. I had taken English classes in Italy, but they didn't help me; when I got to the U.S. I was lost. It was hard to learn English in California because there were so many Persians that you were always speaking in Farsi. There was Persian radio, Persian TV, Persian newspapers. There was too much Persian going on. I felt like saying, "Why didn't you just stay in Iran?"

Once we came back to New York, I still didn't know much English. I had one or two cousins in school, but there weren't any other Persians. I had to learn English. It wasn't just to get good grades. It was to make friends.

I'm glad I'm here because I have so many new opportunities. I want to become a heart surgeon. If I try, I have a chance, but in Iran I doubt that I'd have a chance because I'm a woman. America is a good place as long as you don't get involved with the wrong people.◆

Glossary

absolute monarch A government headed by a monarch whose power has no limitations.
ayatollah Leader of the Shiite sect of the Muslim religion.
chador Veil worn by Muslim women.
depose Remove from a position of power.
dissident One who disagrees.
dynasty The period during which a certain family rules.
embargo A restriction imposed by law on commerce.
empire A uniting of many countries, territories, and peoples under a single power.
faghi The supreme religious guide in the Islamic religion.
monarch The hereditary head of state; king, queen, shah.
secular Nonreligious; worldly.
shah The title of any of the former rulers of Iran.
socialism Any of various theories or systems of the ownership and operation of the means of production and distribution by society or the community rather than by private individuals, with all members of society or the community sharing in work and production.

For Further Reading

Kelly, Ron, Friedlander, Jonathan, and Colby, Anita, eds. *Irangeles: Iranians in Los Angeles.* Berkeley: University of California Press, 1993.

Farman-Farmaian, Sattareh. *Daughter of Persia.* New York: Crown Publishers, 1992.

Kordi, Gohar. *An Iranian Odyssey.* London: Serpent's Tail, 1991.

Laird, Elizabeth. *Kiss the Dust.* New York: Dutton Children's Books, 1991.

Dorraj, Manochehr. *From Zarathustra to Khomeni.* Boulder, CO: Lynne Reinner Publishers, 1990.

Salehi, M.M. *Insurgency Through Culture and Religion.* New York: Praeger, 1988.

Friedl, Erika. *The Women of Deh Koh.* Washington, DC: Smithsonian Institute Press, 1989.

Guppy, Shusha. *The Blindfold Horse.* Boston: Beacon Press, 1988.

Kahn, Margaret. *Children of the Jihn.* New York: Seaview Books, 1980.

Mahmoody, Betty. *Not Without My Daughter.* New York: St. Martin's Press, 1987.

Index

A
Achaemenid Empire, 7
Allah, 9
Anita, 54–60
Aryan, 12

B
Baha Allah, 28, 31
Baha'i, 14, 15, 38, 40, 43, 50–51
  beliefs of 28–31, 52–3
  feast, 53
  persecution of, 27–28
Bani Sadr, Abolhassam, 17

C
chador, 10, 14
Christianity, 15, 27–28
cosmetics, 19, 57

D
Darius I, 7
dating, restrictions on, 47–48
dress code, 47

E
English, learning, 40, 42, 53, 60
Evelyn, 44–49

F
faghi, 13
family, warmth of Persian, 33, 36

Farsi language, 25, 42, 47, 60

H
hadith, 8, 9
hejab (attire), 13–14
hostages, US 16

I
Imam, 9
Iran-Contra Affair, 17
Islam, 7, 9, 28, 51
Islamic Revolution, 7, 12, 15, 28, 33–34, 45, 51

J
Jews/Judaism, 14, 24, 28, 55
  Orthodox, 45
job
  barring from 41
  loss of, 34, 52

K
Khomeini, Ayatollah, 11–16, 22, 32, 33, 37, 55
Koran, 8, 9, 36

M
Marjan, 26–31
Mayam, 38–43
mojahedin, 23–24
Muhammad, 8, 9, 36
Muslim, 10, 11, 143, 19, 24, 28, 36, 50, 57–58

N
names, changing to emigrate, 46
Navid, 50–53

P
Pahlavi, Reza Shah, 9–10
Pahlavi, Mohammed Reza Shah, 11, 16, 22, 33
Pakistan, escape to, 52
Persia, 7
  becomes Iran, 11

R
Rafsanjani, Hojatolislam Hashemi, 17
Reza, 32–37

S
Safavid Dynasty, 8, 9
Savak, 11, 12
school
  in Iran, 51–52, 57–58
  in U.S., 47

Sepi, 20–25
Sharia (Islamic Law), 13
Shiism, 8, 9, 11, 13
sunna, 8
Sunni Islam, 8, 9

T
television, Iranian 41–42

U
university, barring from, 39

V
Vahid, 50–53

W
women, status of, 10, 11, 37, 57

Z
Zoroastrianism, 7, 8, 15

Acknowledgments
A heartfelt thank you to Manucherhr Derakhshani of the Baha'i National Center and Nina Aminpour without whose assistance this book could not have been written. Thank you also to Alan Lahiji, Shamil Erfanian, and Sara, each of whom took the time to speak to me, but whose interviews could not be included because of spatial constraints.

About the Author
Gina Strazzabosco is an editor and free-lance writer in New York City. She has written three books for young adults.

Photo Credits
Cover © Kim Sonsky; p. 6, 16, 25, 30, 49 © Beatniz Schiller/Int'l Stock Photo; p. 13, 29, 43 © Johan Elbers/Int'l Stock Photo; p. 14 © Bill Wrenn/Int'l Stock Photo; p. 56 © Reuters/Bettman; all other photos © AP/Wide World Photos

Layout and Design
Kim Sonsky